when we settle

jenna carara

when we settle copyright © 2021 by Jenna Carara

Cover and interior art by Katherine Carara Johnson

ISBN: 978-0-578-89432-4

dedicated to
mo, katie, kaitlyn, kaylee, aja, erina, morgan, abby

and all of my beautiful friends

who have experienced

life-changing love
happiness
friendship
heartache
heartbreak

and everything in between

contents:

empty   7

search   51

fulfill   95

empty

in silence you will ponder
who you're meant to be
and what defines you

in weakness you can feel
empty
slowly falling into
dangerous thoughts

stay vigilant
stay strong

it's okay to feel
lost sometimes

what great cost
it feels
to love oneself

i'm so afraid of saying
too much
that i end up not saying
enough

i'll sit and wait
give you another chance

in return you'll say i'm unfair
and never see your own faults
lying there

you gave them everything
in return
they gave only

empty promises

letting go
moving forward
forgetting what's
necessary

can be the hardest part
about love
we were never meant
to have

i'll drink a double
to numb the pain
each night before bed
ever since you left

with only darkness to hold me
loneliness to call and
pointless questions to fill
my tired head

i'd rather you lie
than tell me
you don't need me
it would better
though
if you were honest
and let me free
unfortunately
i don't get to choose
and i'll waste all my time
guessing
which side i'm on
by taking your
confusing cues

in the middle of the night
she wakes up with a heavy chest
gasping for air
then
reaches to her side
to find comfort

instead of warmth
she finds only
cold sheets
and an empty bed

what will he be willing
to give up
to get her back

what will she be willing
to give up
to take him back

when the stakes are raised
feelings strengthen
and vulnerability strengthens alongside
in myself
i'm insecure
second guessing
all the words spoken
all the steps taken

regardless of the actions of another
i feel unstable

afraid of losing
something i don't even have

you act as though
it's a large price to pay
to change your ways
i'll fall prey to your weakness
you've never said those
sweet things
before

whatever he says
make sure it stays
you're too good
for falling for the same
tricks

twice

call me the problem
go ahead
i dare you

you'll cause my earth to crumble
and my heart to shatter

through this
i'll wonder
why it makes you feel superior
to push someone down

i crave silence

the second you caused me to break
replays in my head
vividly
it disrupts my thoughts
and echoes through my head
way too loudly

do i dare stand
a chance
in a world
that never stops changing

i move with it
only to be caught
dragging my feet through puddles
of nostalgia and sadness

heart longing for what once was

and never will be again

you were there
to love
you knew
everything
you were
accepting

the one you loved
ended things
indefinitely
claimed them as dead
refused to look at the
darkness
within
that caused the
foundation
to crack

it's incredible
how we can experience suffering
from something
that never happened

i don't mean much to you
it's painfully obvious
i'll slowly kill myself
thinking about
the pretty pictures
i've painted
of us
in my head

i'll open my heart
then let it bleed
until it's finally empty

then
i'll sit in sadness
wondering how to
fill it
back up

instead of healing
i'll delay
the process
clinging onto
the hope
that you'll change

i see your struggle with
vulnerability
you consistently choose
to avoid
self-reflection

knowing this
i still
can't find
what i could have done
to save
my heart
from hurting
as much as it does now

relationships either end
or continue
endings bring two heartbreaks
usually one worse than the other

now it has been done
it's for the best
and now you need to learn
how to heal
on your own

it's okay don't tell me how you are
i'll continue to avoid
confrontation causing
conversations that always
begin with anticipation and
end in frustration

i'm too afraid to lose you
too terrified to honor
what i might need

i'll have to let you go
to get to where i
should probably be

hearts with time
can heal
even though it's the most
painful
feeling
when they first break

my heart falls into the pit of my stomach
i collapse to the ground
gravity wins
i've become
the product of pain winning
over my heart

heartbreak makes the
whole body bleed
tears the mind to pieces
takes us
outside of our body

it's funny how you can feel completely
surrounded
consumed
connected
and yet so alone

in the peaceful moments
rare but necessary
i become uncomfortable being
silent
with only myself to keep me company

i fear a lonely heart is all i'll ever be

i'm too afraid to fall asleep
i can't face what's in the darkness
of my dreams
my greatest fears come alive
and i wake to find
they surround me still

heart begins to ache
searching for a cure
i run quickly to a familiar place
temporarily fixed
then i feel that ache again
learning once more that
nothing's changed

a natural response to heartbreak and the faults of others
is to blame myself
my deepest fears come forward
unworthy
unloved
unneeded
because it seems much easier
to submit to weakness
than pull myself out of the depths
and simply love myself

somehow
i feel closer to you
when my life
is in fragments
you know how
to pick me up
but then leave me
once i'm put back together
again

she left no physical trace of you
no pictures
t-shirts
letters
if only she could erase you
from her memory, too
although she deserves to feel proud
for coming as far as she has
after the damage you caused

she is free now
so let her go
and don't expect her to come back
because that's the last thing
you deserve

as i was following your voice and
hearing your thoughts
my heart sank

for the first time i realize i'm
the only one hurting
the only one that felt the cold sting
of your manipulative ways

i won't speak

i'll just sit there
swallow my words
and try not to choke
i pick my battles wisely
and i don't have
energy
to lose this one

i don't do well with
implications and expectations
however
it shouldn't be so bold of me
to ask you
what you're
actually thinking

happily i would've waited for you
if only you would have spared me
the inconvenience
of letting me know
how you truly felt

now i'll make it easy
remove myself from the equation
and let you waste
someone else's time

i was fine being alone
i accepted independence
then you came along
and i gave you a chance

foolish of me to take chances
and jump blindly
when i had finally proven
i was enough
for myself

i question fate
was my encounter with you necessary
you interrupted the path
of my life

right now the only conclusions
i draw are
fate is cruel and you
are insignificant
in every way

you were the one
who decided to pursue me
make empty promises
you were also the one
who decided it was too much
decided to step back
and pretended
you hadn't
changed your mind

i just went along
cluelessly

this is the last time
i let anyone else
call the shots
clearly i'm the only one
who's competent

i'm
tired
of
playing
the
game
of
who

can

build

higher

walls

i'm so willing to give you
every part of me
i see all the flags
painted vibrantly
red
                    i'll turn them pink
                    then fade them into white
and yet
i find myself again by your side
with no answer
as to why
i keep this pattern

search

in the stillness she

searches

to find that which fills
her soul

for a moment there's peace
then i wonder
how long until that feeling is
just a memory

it's not my responsibility
to put you back together
my energy is consumed
now that i've decided
i'm worth becoming
a complete version of myself

i don't trust myself to be in love
holding another's heart
feels like a risk
i shouldn't be allowed to take

don't call me fickle
don't call me untrue
when the one that's hurting us
is actually you

the prospect of us fills my head
desperate to attach
i leap forward into harm's way
all i can hope
is that you're leading me on

i'll let myself
get completely torn apart
so that i can get put back together again
in a new
and stronger way

she steadies her breath
now reminded
it's time to do things
on her own

maybe he was there
at some point
but that's irrelevant now

he finds his way
she finds hers
at one moment their paths
will cross
for reasons yet to unfold

i'm still looking for the reasons
i feel the way i do
maybe i will find them
maybe i won't but
that's the thing about feelings
we have them
but sometimes don't know why

i can read the words
running across your mind

don't get attached
don't connect
don't open up
don't get hurt

other words in my mind follow

you deserve to be loved
you deserve to be pursued
great love is worth the risk

the rhythm of my words deserve
to be matched

i'm working on shedding disappointment
i'm removing myself from
the downward spiral
caused by the selfish ways
of others

i can't seem to understand
why life is riddled with such
drastic
and constant disappointment

rather than it just being a season of life
it keeps a consistent presence
that we just learn
to live with

if you agree to stay away
respect my boundaries
trust my judgement
i'll listen and play along

soon after you'll switch
step into a line of defense
call me the villain
and claim your feelings as fact
placing them above
anything i ever feel or say

i promise from now on i won't apologize
for reminding you
my feelings are worth more
than your ego

i am going to learn
who i am
for my own heart's sake

one day
he will finally realize the damage
pain
destruction
carelessness
of his selfish actions

one day
he will stop
playing the victim
making excuses
blaming identity crisis
or anything else
besides his own actions

one day
he will come back
and all we can hope
is that she's strong enough
to turn him down
and continue healing

stay at home all alone
drink the whiskey i bought
and take your survey

you wouldn't want
to miss out on someone
better than me

what are you looking for anyway

if i'm not it

in your arms i felt
peace
safety
tenderness

sometimes it's nice
just to be held

in the daytime
things are the way
they've always been
at night our defenses lower

without words we reveal
a deep desire to feel close
to another

then in the morning
we go back to normal
never discussing the unspoken
need we had for each other
just moments before

i'm frustrated with the feeling
of falling for you
it's nothing i asked for
nothing i chose
but now that i'm here
 do i let you know
or do i withhold all
guarding my heart and
stopping
any heartache
before anything gets a chance
to begin

pressed up against me
i feel your heart racing
matching the tempo of mine

put us out of our misery
and just
kiss me already

you'll sit on the sidelines
of reality
doing anything to avoid admitting
what's actually in the depths
of your heart

i won't make time for that
anymore

everyone at some point
mourns the loss
of a love
they never had

in the process
of being honest
all i did was
boost your pride
and kill mine

i struggle to find
the right words

instead of speaking I'm
slowly suffocated
by images of
my greatest fears
coming true

i wonder how it felt
when he decided
to leave
i wonder what thoughts
filled his head
i wonder what lead him
to destroy
thing we both
vowed
to protect

the chase for
perfection
is intoxicating
and addicting
even though it can
never be
reached

every time i think you're gone
forget your face
and erase my memories
you come back
just to tease my affections

once again
like a game
i'll join in and play
and always
let you win

it's magic
when two strangers
in one moment
of meeting
can suddenly speak
as if they met
a long time ago

my life hasn't lost all feelings
of disappointment
i've just better learned how to
live with it

we too often
blame ourselves
when someone
dismisses us
with prejudice
as their only parameter

it's time to realize
it is not our fault
when someone can't see
our beauty
because of the
insecurities
that cloud their vision

set fire to bridges
don't turn back to see the damage
come back later
when the smoke has cleared
and build something
new
stronger
and something that will actually
last

i don't want you to be
just another number
just another face
that passes and then
fades into memory
i pray that you're the one
i spend the rest of my days
loving
holding
and learning

there's potential
for something new
and wonderful to happen

but i shy away
burdened by the past
heartbreaks
feeling the heaviness of the baggage
i never once wished to carry

i want to accept efforts
but i shrink into myself
where i think it might be safer

it's lonely
to be alone

it's safe
to be alone

it's safe
to be alone

it's lonely
to be alone

what are you filling the space
of self-reflection
and self-healing

don't be fooled
by a temporary fix
in the midst of that
more than just you
will be a casualty

someone deserving
finally approaches
how is she supposed to accept
something that life has never
given to her before

making assumptions is a dangerous game
don't ever believe that you are
omniscient enough
to know the heart of another
without hearing them first

no one will ever
understand you
more than your own self
so why are you
denying the opportunity
to get to know
yourself

there is a
delicate balance
between being careful
with your own heart
and letting yourself trust someone
who could care for you
greatly

my mind is my worst enemy
bouncing back between
thoughts of needing you
and thoughts of standing my ground
independently

the most torturous part
is that i don't know which side is right
or which one to lean on to help me
persevere

so i'll just continue swaying from
one thought
to another
becoming progressively
more annoyed with my own voice
inside my head

you're a puzzle i can't quite
piece together
i want to know how invested you are
in me
how often you think of me
when I'm not around

i'm fine with letting you go
because the person you are
is not someone i care to waste
any more time with

what you represented
is a much bigger loss

potential
to finally find a heart
to connect with indefinitely

i can see that could happen now
not with you
but with someone
wonderful
i crave that encounter
and i eagerly await
the day a love like that
arrives

fulfill

she'll find a moment
that sends her heart to great heights
she will be fulfilled by
her own doing
her own healing

give me more than
i can handle
so that i will understand
my strength

i see the faces of the people nearby and
wonder about
paths they've taken
scars on their hearts
the stories that define them
i marvel at the beauty of every person's story that
has led them to the same place as me
at this moment
we might not speak
but we can all know
life is beautiful when you know
you're not alone

someday you will be found
you will be healed
you will be loved
in the way you've always
deserved

maybe it's not what you needed
to hold the rest of your days
instead it was a moment
and a lesson
to push you to the place
where your heart can find
true rest

it took losing
everything
i thought i had
to find
everything
i didn't know
i needed

you need to finally realize
not everyone
gets the pleasure
of knowing
how incredible you are

never underestimate the power
of a tender soft touch
from a person
who values you deeply

it is our nature
to desire
to be held
wrapped in warmth
and safety

how is it possible
that someone can know
exactly what you need
without hearing you
speak a word

with her eyes
she proves patience
with her touch,
she shows affection
with her smile
she opens a world
where she's willing
to share
all that's in her heart

with initiation we give and seek

minutes become hours

in each breath i take
i'm filled with
confidence
in potential
for love that is finally
real

you are worth
so much more than
you've been given

i run my fingers through your hair
memorize every scar on your face
every mark on your heart
all the dreams you've ever had
soaking in every second i get
to be in your presence

i take a deep breath
and wonder what i did
to deserve a love
so sweet and true

everyday
we decide
who to spend our love on

love
isn't an obligation
it's a choice
we consistently make

step into reality
own whatever is yours
and stop
taking on more
than you need

you deserve to feel
all the goodness that is in the world
because you are part of it

your lack of
admiration
desire
and interest
in me
is a loss
you'll regret
forever

as for me i'll move on without
missing a beat

you'll quickly fade into memories
i don't need to recall

we'll close down
the restaurant
not wasting any time
on heart to heart
conversations
that fill me when
i'm empty

sometimes a friend
is exactly what
you need

i won't rest where i am
knowing i'm meant for
so much more

don't ever think
i'm weak
i've found strength
within myself
i'm an immovable force
standing true in things
i believe
backed up by
personal experiences
that reaffirm the person
i am
and who i aim
to be

i won't let
fear collapse me
although it might shake me
i'm done with
falling to its feet

your voice is
worthy
of being heard

i've never felt the ease
of communication
the flow of words
the connection of hearts
more than i have
with you

i'm broken
but not beyond repair

it's so easy
to make something
out of nothing
but this is definitely
a something

and i can't wait to see
what it becomes

may your strength and identity not be
easily disturbed
by forces beyond your control
you were perfectly crafted
to fit into a life
more beautiful than your imagination
can
grasp

we'll talk
the night
onto day

then i'll stall all
responsibilities
just to get
one more second
to be awake
next to you

i caught myself
smiling in my sleep
because the very thought
of you
makes my heart full

i have begun to
acknowledge my worth
independently

regardless of the actions
of others
i'll stand resilient

the very thing
that rips you to shreds
can someday
be the thing
that reminds you
of the strength you have
to make it through
each day

to hear your laugh
to see your smile
to feel your presence
with no obligations
or expectations

to just be myself
how completely
loved
i will feel

i pace my apartment
heart swelling
at the memory
of your smile
your laugh
your kiss
repeating in my head

could it be
everything i have
hoped
and prayed for
might now be here
holding my hand

remember
this life of yours
is a unique
and beautiful story

i don't want to sleep
and make it a new day
i'd rather live here
forever
with the feel of your
touch
as new as it can possibly be

every time i think of you
butterflies cover every inch of me
from the inside out
i'm glowing

my heart warms up
at the thought of your name

one look at you
and i can see the story
of our entire lives
unfolding
in the depths of your eyes
i'm not afraid
i'm home

it takes courage
to be
yourself

i want to taste
your smile
and study
your lips
with mine

the world needs you
exactly as you were created to be

maybe all you'll be
someday
is just a few words
on a page of a book
i decided to write

www.ingramcontent.com/pod-product-compliance
Lightning Source LLC
Chambersburg PA
CBHW031137090426
42738CB00008B/1118